How To Interview A Sleeping Man

50
Hilarious & Heart-Warming Hints
To Help You Save Your Family Memories

from renowned family biographer,

Milli Brown

stories compiled by karey mackin

Illustrations by m. Loys Raymer
Book Design by fit to print
Edited by Mark Murphy

Dedication

"You never get over being a child,
long as you have a mother to go to."
<small>SARAH ORNE JEWETT</small>

I hope I can continue to be a child for many years to come.
Thanks, Mom.

I love my job as the owner of Personal Profiles, a company that helps families preserve their memories. Listening to family stories is fascinating to me because they so often prove to be more exciting than any soap opera anyone could ever write.

But it hasn't always been easy—challenging might be a better word. There have been times when I thought I'd have to give up. In the beginning, there wasn't a "BIOGRAPHY 101" course I could take, nor were there any books on the market that prepared me for the squabbles, equipment problems, last-minute cancellations, and storytellers who can't say "The End."

So I've come up with the answer, a book designed to save you and your family from my mistakes and uneasy forays into the unknown.

N ow that you understand the reasons behind this book, you're probably asking, "Why the title? What does a sleeping man have to do with *my* family history?" Believe me, every history-gathering adventure will probably include a "sleeping man" in one form or another. Maybe it won't be like my sleeping man, but you will no doubt confront resistance of some kind when you launch a project of your own. Let me tell you the story, then I know you'll understand...

A woman asked me to do her husband's biography, and we scheduled his first interview right away. She had been trying for years without success to convince him to write his memoirs, and she had almost given up when she heard about Personal Profiles.

"You're my last hope," she pleaded.

I could have used some help when I showed up with my recorder and a long list of questions for a man who obviously wasn't pleased to meet me and certainly not ready to talk.

"Am I a surprise?" I whispered to his wife.

"A surprise? Hmmm, oh no, definitely not a surprise—hmmm, well, yes, I guess you might be a surprise! Well, I'll just leave the two of you to get to know each other."

And with that, she was gone.

Fortunately, my newest client was too polite to throw me out.

"You just sit back in your favorite chair and get comfortable. We're going to have fun," I assured him.

*B*ut he had a unique way of showing his displeasure as I got ready to proceed with the interview. Before I could ask a question, I was startled to see that he was asleep...or was he pretending?

I had no idea what to do. This was my first interview. I was teetering on the brink of failure just as my career was getting started.

I coughed rather discreetly. Didn't work. I tapped the recorder's microphone and said rather loudly, "Testing—one, two, three—testing." There was no response. So I waited, and waited, and waited some more. Slowly, one eye popped open to see if I was still there. I was, and the interview began. I pulled out all the stops to make that session an enjoyable experience for my clever friend, hoping to keep him inspired until all of his stories were recorded.

His wife and I later laughed about his reluctance, especially when we recalled his rapid change of attitude. She said he had soon come to look forward to our weekly appointments with childlike excitement, and was extremely disappointed when the process was finally completed.

*D*id I wave a magic wand? Not at all. But I was able to ask questions that quickly took my client into memorable episodes of his life, arousing in him an appreciation for the story he had to tell. He came to the same realization that many others have arrived at since the day he "fell asleep" on me:

> Our lives are a treasure not to be forgotten. They should be preserved for those who follow.

My encounter with the sleeping man wasn't my last brush with reluctance, of course. In almost every situation, I've had to discover new ways to make my clients and their families understand the importance of recording their stories and, maybe more importantly, find ways to make the process enjoyable. I try to help them realize that the times of their lives, the great triumphs, personal tragedies, and simple pleasures, are well worth passing on to those who will want to know "why am I who I am, and who came before me?"

*W*hy do I do what I do? And why do I love doing it? Read on, dear reader, for here are fifty of the many reasons why…

Disclaimer

Any similarity to you or your family is just coincidence. Names and stories have been altered to protect the privacy of my cherished clients, as well as the not-so-innocent and not-so-perfect families.

Onto the hints...

Hint One

Watch *It's A Wonderful Life*,
my favorite movie of all time,
and really listen to its message:
Everyone's life *does* matter.

*J*ust a few months ago, I eavesdropped on a conversation between a mother and her daughter as they waited for their appointment in Personal Profiles' reception area. It warmed my heart.

"I don't even know why we're here. My life hasn't been anything out of the ordinary. I didn't go to school. I've never worked...I don't deserve a book, sweetheart."

"Mom, your life is special to *me*. I want to know what it was like for you growing up. Did you fall in love with Dad on your first date? How did you feel when you learned you were pregnant with me? What about when I was expecting your first grandchild? I want my children to know their grandmother. Mom, *your* history is *our* history. Maybe you don't think you deserve a book about your life...but, don't we?"

So many of those I interview, especially women, are simply too modest. They can't believe that their lives have been meaningful enough to record for their families, that anything less than a life of heroic proportions isn't worth preserving. They couldn't be more wrong.

The following quote by Ralph Waldo Emerson is my favorite definition of success:

"To laugh often and much, to win the respect of intelligent people and the affection of children; to earn the appreciation of honest critics and endure the betrayal of false friends; to appreciate beauty, to find the best in others, to leave the world a bit better, whether by a child, a garden patch, or a redeemed social condition, to know even one life has breathed easier because you have lived. This is to have succeeded."

Hint Two

Never interview more than one person at a time.
If the laughing, shouting, and arguing don't
make you crazy, listening to the tape recording will!

*W*hen I began my career as a biographer, I was commissioned by a large family to record their stories. My initial meeting with them could be best described in two words: sheer pandemonium! I was there to do a simple outline for their book. They proceeded to introduce some nasty skeletons who were best kept in the closet. After two hours of absolute chaos, there was no progress. It was only later, when I listened to my tape, that I realized how dreadful it really was.

Here's a sample for your entertainment:

> "I *do* remember why your uncle wasn't invited. He had just lost two of our biggest clients because he was drunk all the time…"

> "That was a horrible time. I don't even want to think about it. If you insist on putting it in the family book, then I want no part of this."

> "I can't believe you just called me a drunk in front of our mother!"

> "Well, you were a drunk."

> "He's right…we didn't know if you'd ever stop drinking. Who knew?"

> "I'm leaving. I want no part of this."

Now I'm a believer that three's a crowd, and I say watch your step even with two.

Hint Three

**Don't rely on oral traditions.
Stories tend to change and fade with time.**

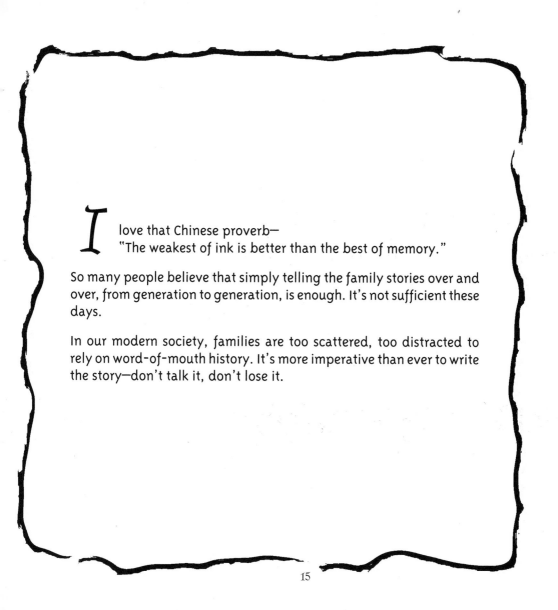

I love that Chinese proverb—
"The weakest of ink is better than the best of memory."

So many people believe that simply telling the family stories over and over, from generation to generation, is enough. It's not sufficient these days.

In our modern society, families are too scattered, too distracted to rely on word-of-mouth history. It's more imperative than ever to write the story—don't talk it, don't lose it.

Hint Four

Be sensitive to memory loss— including *selective* memory loss!

I figured out fast that my client was hard of hearing. So I slipped a little closer, sat face-to-face with him, and raised my voice just a tad. Problem solved. But another problem wasn't so easily understood.

"Now, what year was it that you entered the army?"

"I don't know—*you* look it up!"

Each time I sought clarification on a date, name, or event that he didn't remember as well as he thought he should, he snapped at me, punctuating his replies with very colorful language. (Most of which didn't make it into the book.)

Then it dawned on me. He was simply embarrassed about possible memory loss. I've seen the same behavior in some of my other clients since then, so at the first sign of sensitivity, I've learned to concentrate on the times they *do* remember. Don't dwell on dates.

Now, selective memory is a different story. For a few of my clients, second and third marriages (not to mention a fourth or more) presented problems all their own. Quite simply, dates often didn't add up between a divorce and a new relationship.

I quickly learned to read between the lines of their stories—it's all right to blur those specifics a bit.

Hint Five

**There's no need for diligent fact-checking
in a family history, unless you're planning to see it
on the shelves at your local bookstore.
If it's just for the family, go with the flow.**

A woman, who desperately wanted to be a client, seemed intriguing when she told me about her experiences as a child star, performing "Twinkle, Twinkle, Little Star" on *The Ed Sullivan Show*.

That was exciting stuff, but my fascination soon turned to utter disbelief.

She babbled on about playing baseball with Joe DiMaggio, boxing with Muhammad Ali, shooting baskets with the Harlem Globetrotters, attending church services with Jacqueline Kennedy, singing with Barbra Streisand, dancing with Michael Jackson, having a nightcap with Richard Nixon, marching with Martin Luther King. Needless to say, it would have been too much history...even for me!

There's a difference between genealogy and family history. Genealogy, for the most part, is about names, dates, and places, while family history puts a face on the names, a reason to remember the dates, and a story about the places. Allow a little leeway for creativity.

My tip to you: Listen to outrageous stories, smile at outright tales— *unless* they're as outlandish as the above example. This is *their* family history...as *they* perceive it!

Hint Six

**Before you begin,
target those uncomfortable subjects
that shouldn't be discussed.**

Some of my clients have successfully blocked out terrible memories that they don't want to resurrect. Forging ahead, not acknowledging the pain, will quickly end the interview.

One woman had a horrifying childhood and wanted to start her life story after her sixteenth birthday. So her book began with birth dates and family names, general information that requires recording anyway.

However, the most telling statement in her book reads,

> "I was sixteen when my aunt and uncle rescued me. They took a genuine interest in my well-being. With that change in environment and the concern people started showing for me, my real life began. I never looked back."

Listen to your instincts because knowing what *not* to ask sometimes is the key to obtaining answers to the truly crucial questions.

Hint Seven

Almost everyone becomes nervous
at the sight of a RECORD button,
so be prepared and keep your equipment simple.

When I started interviewing, I thought I needed the best and most expensive equipment, so I ordered a special recorder. It was so advanced that I believed it could almost do the interviews for me! As it turned out, I never even learned to use it properly. And I've been let down too many times by battery-operated models, so all you really need is something simple that plugs into a wall.

One woman became very nervous during one of those early interviews when I used the fancy machine. She kept fiddling with her microphone. On off on off on off. Imagine those transcripts.

"I—CLICK—when I was—CLICK...you just wouldn't believe how I—CLICK—I never told anyone about—CLICK."

Uh oh. The more complicated the equipment, the more that can and will go wrong!

Also, make sure your equipment works properly in the first place, and have a backup plan if it doesn't. I once interviewed a man who started talking the second I walked in the door. I had a good tape recorder, but for some reason it kept getting stuck after each rotation. I had to keep tapping it with a finger to get it going again.

Those transcripts were a nightmare, too. The recorder stopped working just as my client was explaining the intricacies of his business. I missed the last ten minutes, and had to buy two books about the insurance industry to fill in the blanks!

Hint Eight

Feel free to add creativity to your history with an audio or video production— but make sure to stage a dress rehearsal!

I had a client who lived in a small apartment in a retirement community. She had been a concert pianist and still played an organ with gusto and flair at ninety years of age. Her endurance wasn't great, of course, but she agreed to record a performance as a supplement for her book, an appealing bonus for her family.

I started my recorder, "Testing, testing," gave her the signal to begin, and she was off with a flourish. She raised her hands and began to play what looked like a most dramatic rendition of somebody's masterpiece. There was no sound! Silence reigned as her fingers flew across the keyboard, and I didn't have the heart to stop her.

If I had checked her organ at the same time I tested my equipment, I would have understood that she always played in the "silent mode," with the sound piped through her headphones so as not to disturb her neighbors. A flip of the switch would have saved the day.

Hint Nine

Don't begin an interview with painful memories.

One of my very first clients was a woman who alone held her family's full history. Her granddaughters enlisted my help in capturing the life stories of this special person, but they also had an additional request.

Their father died when they were very young, so they had no real memories of him other than a few old photos and documents. The only person who could help them know him was his ninety-year-old mother. Like most families, they rarely talked about their tragedies, so they hoped that an outsider could piece together a picture of the man they never got to know—their dad.

The first interview went very well until the conversation turned to the deaths of the grandmother's husband and two sons, her only children. At the time, I didn't know how to steer an interview away from such tragic topics in time. After such an emotionally draining first interview, I suspected that my client wouldn't want to continue.

She and I still talk on the phone and exchange notes, and she always hints that she might want to try it again. But time is growing short, and with each passing day memories can sadly slip away. I think about that family often and hope that I'll have one more chance to preserve their history.

Hint Ten

Take the phone off the hook,
put a Do Not Disturb sign on the door—
whatever it takes to discourage interruptions.

"OK, Madalyn, I think we can begin now."

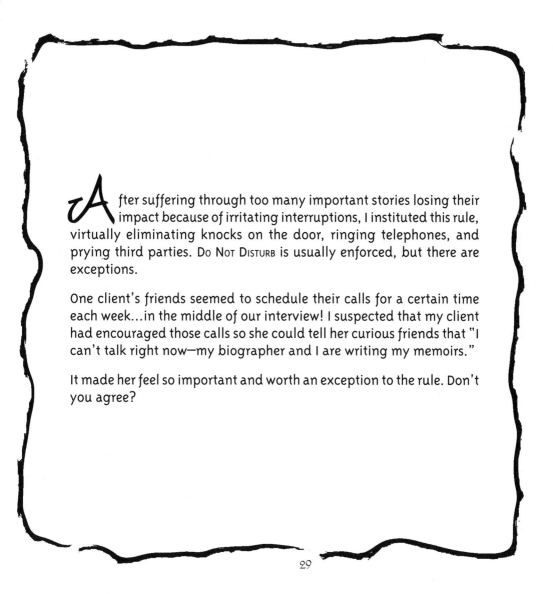

*A*fter suffering through too many important stories losing their impact because of irritating interruptions, I instituted this rule, virtually eliminating knocks on the door, ringing telephones, and prying third parties. Do Not Disturb is usually enforced, but there are exceptions.

One client's friends seemed to schedule their calls for a certain time each week...in the middle of our interview! I suspected that my client had encouraged those calls so she could tell her curious friends that "I can't talk right now—my biographer and I are writing my memoirs."

It made her feel so important and worth an exception to the rule. Don't you agree?

Hint Eleven

**Don't be caught napping
when it comes to sensitive situations.**

When one of my Jewish clients died, I brought his biography to the services, hoping somebody would read from it. Then I remembered everybody's favorite chapter, the "Peanuts and Popcorn" story.

"I had two little pigs, one named Peanuts and the other one Popcorn. My son and daughter loved those pigs, which grew to be about three hundred pounds. Finally I had to take them to a meat packer and turn them into pork chops and ribs. The kids didn't know that I had done this. My daughter came running up, 'Daddy, Daddy! Peanuts and Popcorn are loose!' I said, 'No kidding? Well, look around the neighborhood and see if you can find them.' And of course, they couldn't. One day after dinner, Annie, our cook, brought in this big platter of ribs. She said, 'Here you go, Peanuts and Popcorn!' My God, you should have heard the screaming and crying. I said, 'Don't be silly,' and bit into one of the pork chops. I chewed and chewed, but I just couldn't swallow. That's the story of Peanuts and Popcorn."

Well, I sat in those services and held my breath, suddenly realizing that no one should read that story. Sure, the book was a great tribute to a great man, but this wasn't the time or the place for stories about eating pork.

Hint Twelve

**Do your homework
before you start asking questions—
know what's important and what isn't.**

$\mathcal{A}$ friend asked me to interview her father, who would be in town for a short visit. My time with him would be limited to just one hour, with no opportunity for preparation—I plunged right in.

He was just like the rest of us when we look at our lives, pondering the choices we make in a lifetime, curious as to what might have been had we taken a different path.

I couldn't get a handle on what had really mattered to him. Time was growing short when I shifted the conversation to his wife of forty years who had recently passed away, and his four children. Suddenly, he glowed.

Let me share two excerpts from his book to better convey this man's deepest feelings:

> About his wife: "I don't know when I knew I loved her...somehow, I can't remember a time when I didn't love her."

> About becoming a father: "When the nurse left the hospital room, and we were alone with Max, the first thing we did was take off his shirt and diaper and have a real good look at that little naked baby. He was ours, and he belonged to us both, and it was just a divine moment. We loved it."

I wish we could have talked more, but the lesson learned is to do your homework before you do a history, making sure that you emphasize the most meaningful events in a lifetime.

Hint Thirteen

When interviewing a relative, do not interrupt and
never contradict what is being said
unless you want the conversation
to come to a screeching halt.

*D*aughters, please beware when interviewing your mothers. No matter how much you love each other, this can be dangerous territory, especially if Mom's memory is challenged.

One reason why my service has been so successful is that my interviewers—always an impartial third party—have no emotional bias, and they accept the responses of an individual without expressing doubt.

My understanding was reinforced when I finally interviewed my own mother. Milli A. Brown, family biographer, quickly turned into Mildred Alberta Brown, daughter of Elsie Brown. Gone was the professional interviewer, and in her place sat a person who struggled to remain impartial and unemotional.

My mother reminisced about her childhood, and I bit my lip and hoped she wouldn't see the tears in my eyes. When she told me about her little sister's death, my mother shared for the first time how she somehow felt responsible because she hadn't protected her. I wanted to stop, console her, and make her understand that it wasn't her fault.

Even when I didn't totally agree with her version of events, even when it was painful for me to hear the truth, I had to force myself to let her keep talking. I could not interfere with her memories, which formed our family history. She loved it, and so did I. After years of interviewing other people, I now have a new "favorite" client.

Hint Fourteen

I dare you. Open an old photo album and
try to identify names, dates, and places.
It's hard to do without labels, isn't it?

"That's definitely either my uncle Jack or your great aunt Helen."

$\mathcal{B}$elieve it or not, I buy old family albums at antique auctions and estate sales. Can you imagine a stranger buying your family photographs? Almost all of the photos in these albums are not labeled. Who knows, I might have some of your family members in my nameless, dateless collection. It's all too easy for your ancestors to quickly become strangers.

One of my clients became increasingly upset as we looked through his family photos together. He couldn't attach names to faces—even his grandparents! This was so irritating to him that he wanted to stop. I told him, "Let's continue so that *your* grandchildren will know who *you* are." He did, and they will.

Hint Fifteen

"Milli, I'm not a writer."
Can you talk? Well, then you can write.

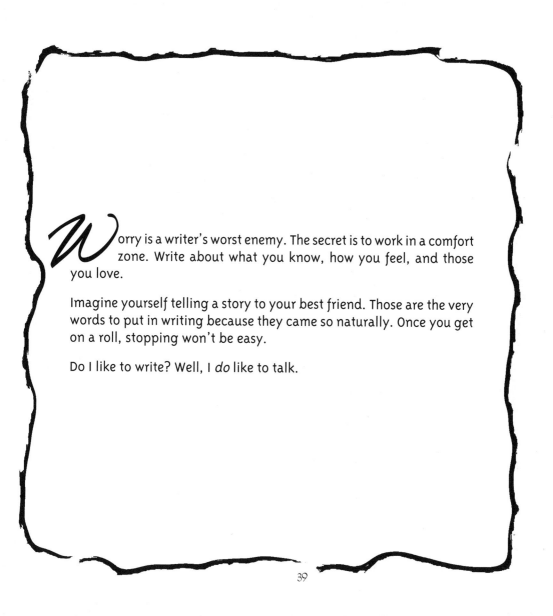

*W*orry is a writer's worst enemy. The secret is to work in a comfort zone. Write about what you know, how you feel, and those you love.

Imagine yourself telling a story to your best friend. Those are the very words to put in writing because they came so naturally. Once you get on a roll, stopping won't be easy.

Do I like to write? Well, I *do* like to talk.

Hint Sixteen

Don't risk failure with plans for long interview sessions. A single, thoughtful encounter is usually enough for most people to tell their stories, especially those who are retired.

I've had a few interviews put on hold because of travel plans or health-related problems. And I must admit to being more than a little skeptical the first few times I was given a last-minute cancellation because of surgery, shingles, a new set of teeth, or a trip out of town. But the excuses always proved to be 100 percent legitimate.

Remember, all of us have a rhythm to our lives, and older people tend to adhere much more closely to their routines than most of us. Favorite television shows, reading the newspaper, nap times, and coffee breaks are daily events that are regulated like clockwork. The answer is a quick, to-the-point interview done on a schedule accommodating these activities.

Also, freedom is one of the many benefits enjoyed by the older generation, and travel is high on their agendas. I'm happy to wave good-bye when they pull the Airstream out of the driveway and cruise into the sunset. They'll have a new story to tell me when they get back.

Hint Seventeen

Know when to allow the conversation to ramble.

I listened quietly while one of my clients talked at length about her family's anguish after her mother slipped into a coma, and it became obvious to them that she was far too ill to continue staying at home. Most of my client's words would never make it into her book, but I knew it was important to let her continue.

I had almost turned off the recorder, and then we got to what I had been looking for, that jewel of a memory that made all the listening worthwhile.

"One day I asked the nurse whether my mother could hear our conversations," she told me.

"Most people don't believe it's possible, but I do," said the nurse.

Well, she began to talk to her mother, reminiscing about their happy times together, thanking her for always dressing her so beautifully.

"I asked Mother, 'Do you remember that pink crêpe de chine dress with accordion pleats? I wore that big layered white hat with a pink rose in it.' And do you know what, Milli? Tears started running down Mother's cheeks. She knew."

It was one of those poignant moments when I knew, too—why I love doing biographies.

Hint Eighteen

Be ready with some light-hearted questions.

*W*ho would you invite to a fantasy dinner party? If you could be somebody else, who would that be? If you won a $40 million lottery, what would you do?

I love to spice my interviews with such questions because they are relaxing and revealing at the same time.

I asked one of my clients, an eighty-something widow, to describe the happiest day of her life. I loved her answer.

> "A year before we got married, Frank told me we could tie the knot as soon as he could save one thousand dollars. I thought, That'll be so long that by the time he saves that much money, I won't be able to walk down the aisle. But sooner than expected, I got a telegram from him that said, 'Just made the thousand dollars. STOP. Will you marry me? STOP.' I think the happiest day of my life must have been when Frank finally made that thousand dollars."

Hint Nineteen

Before videotaping a family history,
do a thorough study of timing and surroundings—
take note of any possible distractions.

I was videotaping a segment for my *Do-It-Yourself Video Biography Kit*, and I selected a serene, beautiful spot for the location. This was my favorite place to relax in the evenings, where I would read and quietly savor the end of a busy day. I loved the large trees and the cascading fountains in the ponds nearby. And who could resist my neighbor's large, lovable dogs who knew I would bring them a treat before darkness fell?

We set up the taping for mid-afternoon, and as I began to arrange for the shoot, I suddenly noticed a few things. The trees were full of noisy birds, the fountains drowned out my voice, and the dogs were not nearly ready for bedtime, barking expectantly—where was their treat? I also could hear honking horns from the busy street and the traffic 'copter overhead. This was tranquility?

I learned my lesson, of course. You must check every detail when choosing a location for your video message, including the noise factor at a certain time of day.

Oh, and we ended up filming inside.

Hint Twenty

Leave room for vanity—
we've all been there before.

There's no age limit to vanity! One of my clients wanted to delete any indication of her age (eighty-something) from her biography. Sounds simple enough until you consider all of the other dates that needed to be altered—the year she graduated from high school, how old she was when she married, her age when her children were born, and numerous other indicators of her age. She even selected a cover photo taken a decade earlier.

That reminds me of my favorite Hallmark commercial where two women attending their friend's 100th birthday party whisper conspiratorially to each other, "You know, she's really 101."

Hint Twenty-One

Be sensitive to blended families.

No matter what the relations are between first and second wives or children from different marriages, don't allow any negative feelings to tarnish a family's precious history.

One client didn't want his third wife in his memoirs. After long discussions with him, he reluctantly agreed to include her, but he also wanted to mention some very nasty things. That wouldn't work, of course, but I finally got through to him when I said:

> "No matter what your feelings are for that woman, you created a wonderful child together, someone you love dearly. Think about *her* when you talk about her mother."

I was in the middle of an interview with another client when our conversation turned to his first wife, who had died a few years earlier. Suddenly, his second wife—who I didn't even know was in the house—interrupted us, calling out from I-don't-know-where that they had plans and were running late. There were apologies, and the situation was handled without a fuss, but we both knew that his second wife was still more than a bit jealous of his lasting love for his first wife.

These can be difficult situations if not handled with kid gloves. Remember, there's no room for spite in a family history. Think of how stubbornness or jealousy might affect the perceptions of generations to come.

Hint Twenty-Two

Don't let anyone discourage you.

It was a box full of letters and speeches, unorganized and fading rapidly. To my friend, it was a treasure left by his mother and only recently discovered. He was rightfully excited and wanted to push ahead with a book full of her writings, honoring her accomplishments and acknowledging the difference she had made in many lives.

He grew emotional several times as we talked, and I assured him I could help. Two days later, after he spoke to his sister, he informed me that we would have to put everything on hold indefinitely. His sister didn't think the project was worthwhile, explaining, "We know what she meant to us, and that's enough for me." Sadly, I don't think it was enough for him, and I wonder where those letters will be in twenty years?

Not everyone will bring the same enthusiasm you have to a family history effort. Some will be reluctant to talk. Others might refuse to help. But if you persevere, support might come along and surprise you.

Hint Twenty-Three

Someone once said,
"Memories are like snowflakes—
no two are ever the same."
They were right.

I've interviewed so many family members who have described drastically different versions of the same event. Whose version should I go with? I finally came to a wise conclusion—that's not for me to decide.

I always laugh when I recall one family's varied memories of Christmas 1978. The young couple had just moved to a new home, far away from parents and siblings. With great anticipation, they invited their families to visit. So the wife's mother, father, and two sisters made the 800-mile trip by car. Along the way they argued, stopped speaking to each other, and were not a jolly group upon arrival.

The husband's family—Mom, Dad, three brothers, their wives, and a herd of nieces and nephews—showed up full of good cheer and gifts galore. But soon they weren't speaking to their son. Seems they were more than a little miffed about staying at a hotel while "her" family stayed at the house.

Imagine the differing memories of that couple's first Christmas in their new home. My advice is take a positive view when interviewing a family. It's fun to compile all the different versions. I call it flavoring the soup.

How did Christmas 1978 end? About an hour after everyone left, the couple had nearly forgotten the debacle when the doorbell suddenly rang. There stood the wife's father with a sour look on his face.

"Mother forgot her coat."

Hint Twenty-Four

If you're interviewing both Mom and Dad and
combining their stories into one book,
be cautious when asking similar questions.

*C*ouples fascinate me by the way they assume compatible but different roles in their partnerships. One of them will be great at remembering details while the other is adept at capturing emotions involved in the same event.

In a memorable interview I asked the wife if she remembered her first date with her husband.

"I certainly do," she replied. "I had met one of his friends soon after college started, and he introduced us in class one afternoon. Our first date was on a Sunday night, and we were with two other couples. None of us knew what to do, but the boys were in suits so we really couldn't do anything casual. We were undecided on a movie, so we went back over to my house and played some parlor games. It was a very enjoyable time."

Than I asked the husband how he felt the first time they met.

"I was sitting with a friend of mine when in walks this girl. I don't know what it was, but I saw her and looked at my friend and I asked him, 'Do you know her?' He said, 'Yeah, do you want to meet her?' I said, 'I sure do.' Love at first sight? It had to be. I had never had anything hit me like that before or since. She's my life."

If you are quick to understand the different personalities of couples you interview, you can go straight to their strengths by carefully phrasing tailor-made questions. Let your instincts be your guide.

Hint Twenty-Five

When you're videotaping, watch out for windows!

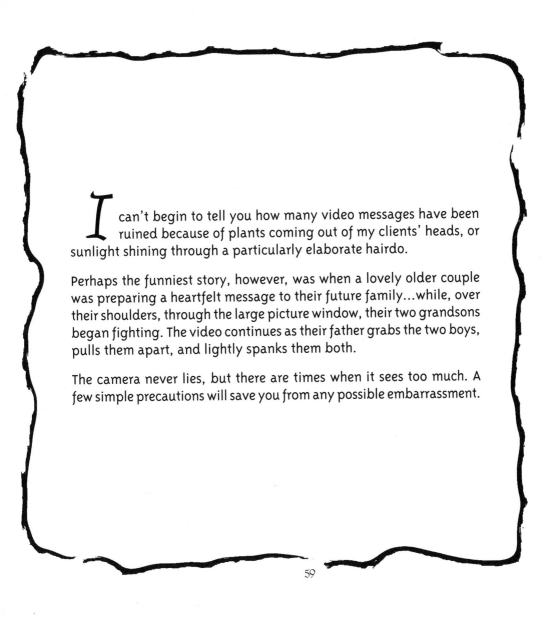

I can't begin to tell you how many video messages have been ruined because of plants coming out of my clients' heads, or sunlight shining through a particularly elaborate hairdo.

Perhaps the funniest story, however, was when a lovely older couple was preparing a heartfelt message to their future family...while, over their shoulders, through the large picture window, their two grandsons began fighting. The video continues as their father grabs the two boys, pulls them apart, and lightly spanks them both.

The camera never lies, but there are times when it sees too much. A few simple precautions will save you from any possible embarrassment.

Hint Twenty-Six

Everyone can have a bad day.

$\mathcal{B}$e a pillar of patience, dealing kindly with bad moods, complaints about aches and pains, the fallout from family issues and arguments. Remind yourself that you're about ten minutes away from brightening somebody's day. (See Hint Forty-Three.)

I have always believed the most precious virtue is patience, and it is the most difficult of all to practice.

Hint Twenty-Seven

Don't record only the big moments in your lifetime.
Often, the most dramatic occasions are
fleeting glimpses of love and kindness.

$\mathcal{A}$ friend told me about coaching his five-year-old son's first soccer game. The child was so frightened that he wouldn't let go of his father's leg! He wanted his dad to go out on the field with him and hold his hand during play.

My friend was smiling, but he made a comment I'll never forget:

> "I'd love for him to know about that day—the pride and the sadness I felt when he finally let go of my hand—but that's one of those memories that probably will slip through the cracks."

I hope that doesn't happen. His son shouldn't be deprived of that special story.

Make sure you write it down...so you can hand it down.

Hint Twenty-Eight

**Don't procrastinate.
It's always later than you think
when it comes to collecting memories.**

$\mathcal{A}$ man commissioned me to write his father's biography. It was clear that the bond between the father and son was strong, especially when I discovered that the dad, a doctor, had delivered his son on his own birthday.

The father lived in another state, but he always traveled to Dallas in the fall for a Cowboys' football game, so his son gave him a Personal Profiles' gift certificate. Included were the dates of his scheduled interviews months later, as arranged by the son.

> "No hurry," he told me when I questioned the delay. "Dad will be here soon enough, and we can get to work then. He's really looking forward to this, and so am I."

He called me a few months later and said that his father had passed away. To this day I hate to hear the words, "No hurry."

Hint Twenty-Nine

**Warning! Don't show anyone that first draft
until you know it's safe for all eyes.**

It was one of the worst days of my life.

I want my clients to see drafts of our Personal Profiles to check for accuracy. In this particular case, I wanted my client to carefully look again at how he had accounted for his previous marriage—dangerous territory in any family history. I told him of my misgivings and left a transcript of his interview with him so he could go over these most sensitive areas.

A few days before Christmas, his son called me and said, "My stepmother is in the hospital. They think she's had a heart attack."

"What happened?" I asked.

"Well, you know that transcript you gave Dad? He left it lying on the coffee table."

Hint Thirty

Libel, invasion of privacy,
defamation of character...don't underestimate
the power of the written word.

"But, your Honor...I swear I edited the really bad stories!"

$\mathcal{B}$e a responsible interviewer by weeding out gossip and innuendo, meanness and revenge. One of my clients, a powerful Hollywood attorney, loved to recall outrageous cases, and I made ample use of an editor's best friend: the PAUSE button.

One of his stories went something like this:

> "His name was—PAUSE—but I'll just call him Mr. X. His wife was an alcoholic, and she took tons of pills. He was a fat slob, and she was a real chic-looking gal...much younger than he was. He wanted a divorce because he couldn't take any more of her drinking and raising hell. He came to see me, and I filed a suit for divorce. The day the case was set for trial, her side had filed motions to continue the case because of her health. The judge said, 'You're going to have to have some doctor swear that she's in poor health.' So they bring her to the courtroom, and she's laid out on a stretcher! Her attorney said, 'Your Honor, my client can't even move! See?' I quickly stood by the stretcher and argued that she was in good health, kicking the stretcher while I talked. Finally, she jumps up and screams, 'Quit kicking this stretcher!' The judge says, 'This case is going to trial.'"

What a juicy story—PAUSE—but nothing to write home about.

Hint Thirty-One

Know what to ask and when to ask it.

*N*ever, "So, tell me about your life...from the beginning, of course."

Always, "Where were your grandparents born?"

Begin with simple, basic questions, then build momentum for more complicated topics later in the interview. I always begin with questions about ancestry, mostly because I'm curious and also because the answers come easily. Reach back a generation or two, then ease yourself into the present and take advantage of the comfort level you will have achieved.

It's as easy as one, two, three. Just think yesterday, today, tomorrow. Establishing a rhythm in an interview makes talking contagious and infects even shy people with the confidence to be more open.

You're learning all my secrets.

Hint Thirty-Two

Control your interview—otherwise, *it* controls *you*.

"Whoops!"

There's a definite difference between unrehearsed conversation and a well-planned interview. I call it chaos vs. tranquility. You need a game plan and an outline. So many people have told me that they sat down to interview their mother or grandfather or great aunt, and then the thought struck, "Uh oh...now what?"

That's why I created a line of do-it-yourself products as guides for families who find themselves in this situation—and to save their sanity as they record their stories! Having a plan also will help you with a family member who has a tendency to digress. I don't have a whistle, but I do tell my clients beforehand, "We're going to be discussing this subject and that subject. Please don't talk about your siblings when we're talking about your mother."

I usually come up with a signal to let someone know if they're straying from the topic. At first, one of my favorite clients would see my "rambling" signal, cover her mouth, and say, "Whoops!" After a time, I didn't even have to signal her. She'd cover her mouth, her eyes would open wide, and she would cry, "Whoops!" She loved to ramble almost as much as she enjoyed beating my signal!

Hint Thirty-Three

Be prepared to change your plans.

I arrived at one client's home with the final proof of his memoirs. He had been in poor health, so I was pleased that we had been able to continue with the interviews and reach a happy conclusion without any breaks in the schedule.

His wife answered the door and said, "You'll never guess what happened last night!" Their first great-grandchild had been born, and my client was elated and rejuvenated. I dashed back to the office for my tape recorder so we could have one more interview to properly end his book.

We talked about the newborn child. This opened the door for questions about his hopes for the boy's future and the advice he'd like to give him. Can you imagine how this child will feel when he reads his great-grandfather's book? He will be a part of this man and know him by the written legacy he has left.

Be willing to open up a closed book and give it a new ending. Stories of a lifetime are treasures, well worth that last touch of polish that gives them the luster they so richly deserve.

Hint Thirty-Four

**Place you and your family in historical context
for the benefit of future generations.**

We'd all like to know what life was like for our ancestors during earth-shaking events that shaped the world. Imagine the early excitement over electricity, telephones, automobiles, and airplanes. The problem is we're losing those who remember such events.

This was why one of my clients decided to write his memoirs.

> "One hundred years from now, people might be traveling to the moon in the same way I travel down the Tollway to downtown Dallas. I can't imagine how my ancestors lived—traveling across country in a covered wagon. I'd love to know how they did it, but I won't because it's buried with them. It's lost forever. I don't want that for my family."

We're living in the greatest age of discovery man has known. Future generations will be very curious about what it was like when man first stepped on the moon, how your life was saved by some great medical advance. Remember, leave footprints your descendants can track.

Hint Thirty-Five

**Don't worry about being politically correct—
you can't rewrite family history.**

A very special client dedicated his book to several women who had dramatically influenced his life. One of those mentioned was Annie, his family's housekeeper and beloved nanny during his entire youth. His family's name for her included a term that was somehow acceptable and commonplace in a different time and region, and I tried to talk him out of using it in his memoirs.

> His wife explained it this way: "Milli, that was what he called her. He loved her as though she was his mother, and he wants to dedicate his book to her."

So he did.

> "Injun Annie was so great, so loving to my family. She was never too busy to wipe the tears away. Her care and help made us survive. She is buried in the family cemetery, and I look forward to the day I'll see her again."

I lost some sleep over this one. But I know that every time my client reads this dedication, he feels proud of his tribute to Annie.

Hint Thirty-Six

Edit wisely, but allow for personality.

I loved talking to one of my clients because he was an uninhibited, colorful storyteller. Sometimes he was a bit too colorful. One of his original transcripts went something like this:

> "My worst habit is cussing, but what the hell do you expect out of a damn truck driver and a sailor? My boy was right when he said, 'Dad, you ain't nothin' but a damn ol' truck driver they put a tie on.' He was right. I'm past the point of trying to impress people. I don't give a damn whether they like it or not!"

After he read a transcript for the first time, he said sheepishly, "I didn't know I was saying damn all the time. You shouldn't have to put up with crap like that, Milli." Frankly, mere words have never phased me, and I knew he had a good editor.

Try to capture the true personality of your subject, but put on your editor's cap and save everybody from embarrassment. Do allow the character and unique language of a family to flavor their history.

Hint Thirty-Seven

**Don't wait until you're ninety
to start recording your life story.**

I think one of my clients explained it best:

> "I wish I had started my memoirs ten years ago. So much has been lost, and so many of my family and friends are no longer around to share this with. So much valuable information has gone with them, and many occasions I can no longer remember—all faded away in just ten years."

Another client summed up perfectly the reason for recording your stories before it's too late:

> "I wanted to do this book for my children, my grandchildren, and my great-grandchildren. I wanted to give them something to reach out and touch. I only wish I had known to start sooner. Everybody has a wonderful story to tell, but who the *hell* gets around to doing it!"

We all procrastinate, but don't risk losing crucial chapters in your book by telling yourself it can wait. Remember, don't put off until tomorrow what you can do today.

Hint Thirty-Eight

Include everyone in the process—
even if you really don't want to.
But remember the old saying,
"Too many chefs will spoil the broth."

I was advising a group of women who were organizing a family reunion. They sent out almost two hundred letters to their relatives requesting memories and stories. They asked me how long to give everyone to return their inclusions—would three weeks be enough?

"Three weeks might as well be three months," I said, "unless you call each person at least five times." I'm *still* waiting for a client's son to send me an updated photograph that I requested over a year ago (you know who you are!).

Hint Thirty-Nine

**Treat your stories and your photographs
for what they are...
treasures worth preserving.**

$\mathcal{A}$ family recently came to us with a finished product. The author had created his work seventy-five years ago, writing at the time:

> "These recollections are not intended to be an autobiography. I do not cherish the delusion that my life has been of sufficient prominence or importance to justify such a record. At a later time, when the curtain has fallen and closed the simple drama of my life, perhaps my children will think it worthwhile to give these recollections a permanent form. It is pleasant to think that in the future my children and my children's children may sometimes be moved to look at what I've written, smile at some of the incidents I have set down, and think tenderly of the hand that recorded them."

I have watched his children's children read his book with pride, confirming once again the value of preserving the thoughts of those who came before us.

Hint Forty

**Don't let a recorder or a camera
come between you and a good story.**

"Shhh!"

One of my clients had a stuttering problem as a child and was still embarrassed as an adult, so he would speak ever so slowly and carefully when I taped our interviews. Then I started to conceal the recorder, allowing him to forget that it was there. He quickly became comfortable, talking at a normal pace, and with a memory that improved as quickly as he relaxed.

My signature books include a taped message for future generations, but no matter how hard I have tried, he won't tape one. Who knows, maybe that old hidden-recorder trick will work again some day. Then his book will be complete.

Hint Forty-One

Don't underestimate the appeal of your book.
Print enough copies to satisfy the demand.

$\mathcal{A}$ client thought he only wanted one book because he didn't believe his family would be very interested and might even think of him as egotistical if he gave them a book about himself.

He changed his mind when I told him what his grandson had said.

"Ms. Brown, can I buy one of Grandpa's books?"

"No," I replied, "but if you ask him, I'm sure your grandfather will gladly give you one."

Look at it this way: Grandparents always have "brag books" full of photos of their grandchildren. Well, Personal Profiles are simply brag books for the grandkids, a great way for them to fully comprehend the richness of the lives their loved ones lived.

Hint Forty-Two

**Don't forget about the animals in your family—
and I don't mean your brother's children!**

"So, tell me...when did you adopt the Wilson's?"

*T*he family pet often is the only one who would talk to you when you were grounded, always had time for you, and always consoled you after an argument. Our relationships with our animals sometimes tell us more about ourselves than our human relationships.

One of my clients is a successful, powerful man who accomplished a great deal in his lifetime and receives abundant recognition. He is surrounded by family and friends, all of whom shower him with love and admiration.

We were selecting photos for his book one afternoon, and he gave me a beautiful formal photograph of himself with his Black Labrador. The caption he chose for that picture?

"My best friend."

Hint Forty-Three

You might start feeling like a do-gooder...
because you really are.

One of my most fulfilling book efforts was with a woman who had lived a life packed full of travel, music, and a circle of friends that spanned the globe. She had never married, had no children, and had no close relatives. She wondered who would care enough to read her story, especially now that she felt so alone in a new retirement community.

"Milli, I feel like an outcast here, a single old woman with a lot of memories but nobody to share them with," she told me. So, I did two things to confirm for this lovely woman that she had indeed lived a full and worthwhile life.

We published her life's history in paperback form, making it easier for her to send to friends in far-off places. Then, we arranged for a book signing, which was attended by a large number of her new neighbors who loved the book.

Near the end of the signing, she leaned over to me and whispered, "Milli, I wish this day could last just two more hours." Make that both of us.

Experts tell me that the process of reviewing one's life is an elixir for the aging, instilling confidence, enhancing self-worth, creating pride in a lifetime of accomplishment. I've seen it with my own eyes, especially in this case.

Hint Forty-Four

Take this opportunity to tell your family things you always wanted to say but didn't.

$\mathcal{U}$nfortunately, many of us can relate to this man's problem:

"I'm ashamed to tell you," my client said, "but I can't remember when my children were little. I would leave home on a Monday morning and wouldn't get back until very late Friday. It was a hard life, but I was doing what it took to eke out a living. I loved the kids, but I was working all the time. It was a matter of survival."

The children's perspective came from another client's son:

"I remember riding in the car with my father every once in a while. I tried to talk fast so I could tell him everything in the little time we had together."

When I relayed this to his father, it prompted him to explain why he had to be away from home so much. He had to support his family, and that meant a lot of time at the office. He had no choice, but he's a terrific grandparent, typical of a father of his generation.

One client used this opportunity to tell his family of his greatest regret in life:

"I'm sorry to say that the night my daddy died, I started over to his house, but I was so angry at him over something we had discussed that I headed into town just to walk it off. Daddy was dead before daylight."

Words of praise or explanation don't have to go unsaid. It's not too late to express true feelings, even for the first time.

Hint Forty-Five

Leave blank pages at the end of the book.

$\mathcal{S}$o many times, when I deliver the finished books to my clients, they read them and then say, "Oh no! I forgot to include the story about the time I..."

It's a lot like the old family Bible, with the birth and death dates of every family member written faithfully through the decades, a never-ending task. Look on your family history the same way. You can't possibly contain all your memories in one book. There will always be more to add.

I encourage my clients to continue recording their memories long after we've finished our time together. Hopefully, I've taught them well.

Hint Forty-Six

Resist the temptation to over-rehearse for a video production...this means no cue cards!

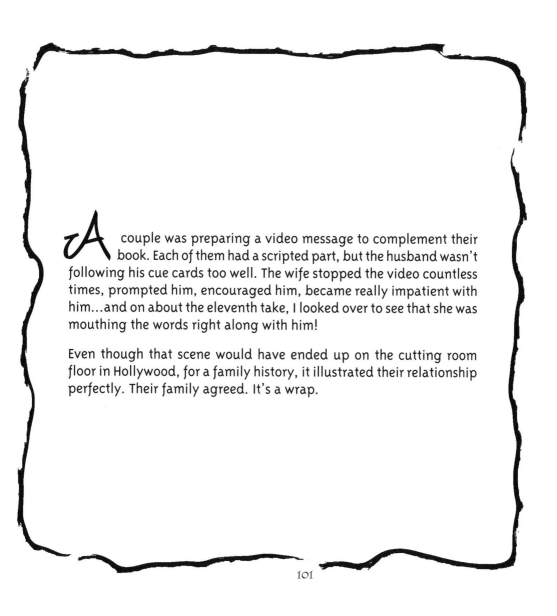

$\mathcal{A}$ couple was preparing a video message to complement their book. Each of them had a scripted part, but the husband wasn't following his cue cards too well. The wife stopped the video countless times, prompted him, encouraged him, became really impatient with him…and on about the eleventh take, I looked over to see that she was mouthing the words right along with him!

Even though that scene would have ended up on the cutting room floor in Hollywood, for a family history, it illustrated their relationship perfectly. Their family agreed. It's a wrap.

Hint Forty-Seven

**Don't be afraid of reliving
the tragic moments of your life.**

With each of my clients, I've learned that the fear of reliving painful memories can inhibit even the most open people. We're all afraid of exposing our strongest feelings, afraid that we might bring back painful times just by talking about them.

When I first met one of my favorite clients, he told me, "Milli, no one has enjoyed life more than I have—no one!" He loved telling me about his happy childhood and his many accomplishments, but his enthusiasm waned as soon as we delved into anything but the best of times.

At first he just dipped a toe in troubled waters until we talked about World War II. As he recalled the day the war ended, he broke down and cried. He told me of his great relief when the news came, and his sadness for the friends he had lost. When he was through, he sat back in his chair and sighed with relief. It wasn't as bad as he thought it would be. And it only got easier.

In the end, he told me something I'll never forget:

"Hell, darlin'—I enjoyed *reliving* my life more than I did *living* it!"

I know it's scary, but remembering yesterday can make today and tomorrow better in so many ways. And, sometimes, it's much easier to review your life because you already know how your stories end. You'll just have to trust me on this one.

Hint Forty-Eight

It's never too late.

eople tell me all the time, "I wish I had heard about you before my dad died." I quickly tell them, "Just because your dad is gone, doesn't mean he has to be forgotten."

I've done many posthumous books for families who lost loved ones before they found me. And I think, in part, that's why I started Personal Profiles. We should be aware that those crystal clear memories of the people who made a difference in our lives might fade with time.

You may have vivid memories of important family members—their personalities, their accomplishments, their impact on your life—but do your children share those insights? The best way to preserve an understanding and respect for those who came before you is to record your thoughts in writing.

We all wonder why we are who we are, why we do what we do. I believe many of the answers lie in having an understanding of past generations.

Hint Forty-Nine

This family history-taking isn't just for older people.

A certain young man teasingly said I talked to old people for a living. Well, I was indignant but nicely asked him a question.

"If I could give you a book about your grandmother, telling you how she was nearly swept overboard during a storm at sea as she and her family traveled to America...how their trunk and most of their belongings were stolen by thieves...how other children made fun of her because she could only speak Italian...how she and her brother sold baked goods door-to-door instead of going to school...how she always argued with a handsome Irish boy in the neighborhood, and married him years later...how she felt the first time she held your father in her arms...and how she felt when you were born...would you like to read that book?"

"I'd love to have that book," he whispered, eyes as big as saucers.

"Well," I told him, "*that's* what I do."

Hint Fifty

**Don't be afraid to finish your family history.
It doesn't mean "The End" of your life.**

$\mathcal{S}$ome of my first clients are *still* working on their biographies! I used to think, "Well, the longer this continues, the better it will be." Not true. I finally realized that if I were them, I also might superstitiously delay putting a closing chapter in my history.

Your book should be freshened, not ended. I encourage my clients to update every year on their birthdays, anniversaries, or upon the birth of a new family member. It's easy. Think about the beginning, forget the ending.

Here's what one client said:

> "After working on my book with Milli Brown for more than three years, I felt some pressure to complete it. That's when I fully realized that through this I've had a rare opportunity to relive my life. I've remembered many of the exciting times. Some of the sad times, too. And the wonderful people from my life—many of them are here. Alive again. Young again. With me. But, of course it's not all in here. It can't be. I'm still living life to its fullest. If you're reading this, I must still be alive in some way."

She quickly concluded her book and promised regular updates.

As for my book, let's just say...to be continued.

91373

Please send me _____ copy(ies) of
How To Interview A Sleeping Man

Price: $17.95 (includes first-class postage)

Send your check or money order to:
Personal Profiles, Inc.
16200 N. Dallas Pkwy., Suite 225
Dallas, Texas 75248

To order with your VISA, MASTERCARD, or AMERICAN EXPRESS, call:
(972) 732-1252

Deliver book(s) to:

Name: _____

Address: _____

City/State/Zip: _____

Telephone: _____

(Please make check or money order payable to Personal Profiles, Inc.)

$\mathcal{D}$ear Reader,

I'd love to hear about your own family history-taking adventures, from your greatest triumphs to your most frustrating fiascos...and even your very own "sleeping man" challenges. Simply write down your stories, along with your name and address, and send them to me.

Who knows, you just might make it into my next book!

Milli A. Brown